Five Senses

THIS EDITION
Editorial Management by Oriel Square
Produced for DK by WonderLab Group LLC
Jennifer Emmett, Erica Green, Kate Hale, *Founders*

Editors Grace Hill Smith, Libby Romero, Maya Myers, Michaela Weglinski;
Photography Editors Kelley Miller, Annette Kiesow, Nicole DiMella;
Managing Editor Rachel Houghton; **Designers** Project Design Company;
Researcher Michelle Harris; **Copy Editor** Lori Merritt; **Indexer** Connie Binder; **Proofreader** Larry Shea;
Reading Specialist Dr. Jennifer Albro; **Curriculum Specialist** Elaine Larson

Published in the United States by DK Publishing
1745 Broadway, 20th Floor, New York, NY 10019

Copyright © 2023 Dorling Kindersley Limited
DK, a Division of Penguin Random House LLC
23 24 25 26 10 9 8 7 6 5 4 3 2 1
001–334112–Sept/2023

All rights reserved.
Without limiting the rights under the copyright reserved above, no part of this publication may be reproduced, stored in or introduced into a retrieval system, or transmitted, in any form, or by any means (electronic, mechanical, photocopying, recording, or otherwise), without the prior written permission of the copyright owner.
Published in Great Britain by Dorling Kindersley Limited

A catalog record for this book
is available from the Library of Congress.
HC ISBN: 978-0-7440-7528-1
PB ISBN: 978-0-7440-7529-8

DK books are available at special discounts when purchased in bulk for sales promotions, premiums, fundraising, or educational use. For details, contact: DK Publishing Special Markets,
1745 Broadway, 20th Floor, New York, NY 10019
SpecialSales@dk.com

Printed and bound in China

The publisher would like to thank the following for their kind permission to reproduce their images:
a=above; c=center; b=below; l=left; r=right; t=top; b/g=background

Depositphotos Inc: Anna_Om 1b, romrodinka 8-9; **Dreamstime.com:** Iryna Kazlova Airspa 14-15, Akulamatiau 7br, Allihays 17bl, Darren Baker 16br, Andrii Borodai 7bc, Charnsitr 13cr, Cherydi 12-13, Gary Cooper 15br, Jose Manuel Gelpi Diaz 19bl, Doxtar 6bc, Gaysorn Eamsumang 9bc, Jordi Mora Igual 14br, 23bl, Laurentiu Iordache 12br, 23clb, Jetzt 17bc, Jkha 9bl, 23cla, Lindas131 13bl, Miceking 11bl, Millafedotova 6br, Monkey Business Images 6-7, Sasi Ponchaisang 19br, Jesse Rodrigues 7bl, Yevgen Rychko 10bc, 23tl, Seventyfourimages 4-5, Thomas Vieth 10-11; **Getty Images:** DigitalVision / Ariel Skelley 19bc, Mikhail Reshetnikov / EyeEm 15bl, Photodisc / Josie Gealer 20-21, Stone / PM Images 18-19; **Getty Images / iStock:** E+ / chpua 16-17, 23cl, E+ / dmphoto 11br, E+ / fstop123 22, E+ / M_a_y_a 21bl, E+ / martinedoucet 9br, E+ / RgStudio 13br, Jacoblund 21br; **Shutterstock.com:** Russamee 17br, Chaiwoot Seetha 18br, Tracy Spohn 20br, Wanida_Sri 8bc, Waridsara_HappyChildren 3cb

Cover images: *Front:* **Dreamstime.com:** Colorfuelstudio cb, Microvone

All other images © Dorling Kindersley
For more information see: www.dkimages.com

For the curious
www.dk.com

Pre-level

Five Senses

Libby Romero

Let's go outside and use our senses!

The human body has five senses.

- see
- smell

Look!
Her eyes can see.
They see the animals.

see

Listen!
Their ears can hear.
They hear the group play and sing the music.

hear

taste

Taste!
Her tongue can taste.
The peach is sweet.

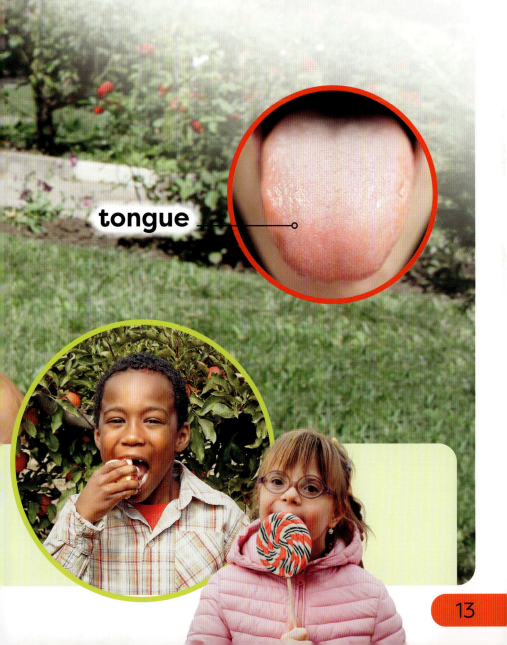

tongue

touch

Touch!
Her fingers touch a soft puppy. Beware of its sharp teeth!

15

Smell!
His nose sniffs.
It smells all
the flowers.

smell

Senses send messages to the brain.
The brain tells the body how to react.

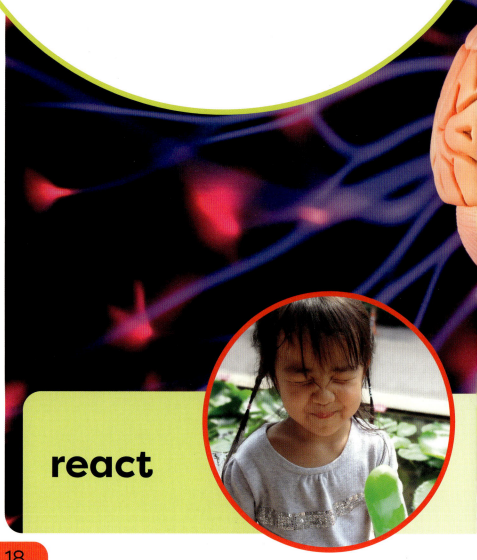

react

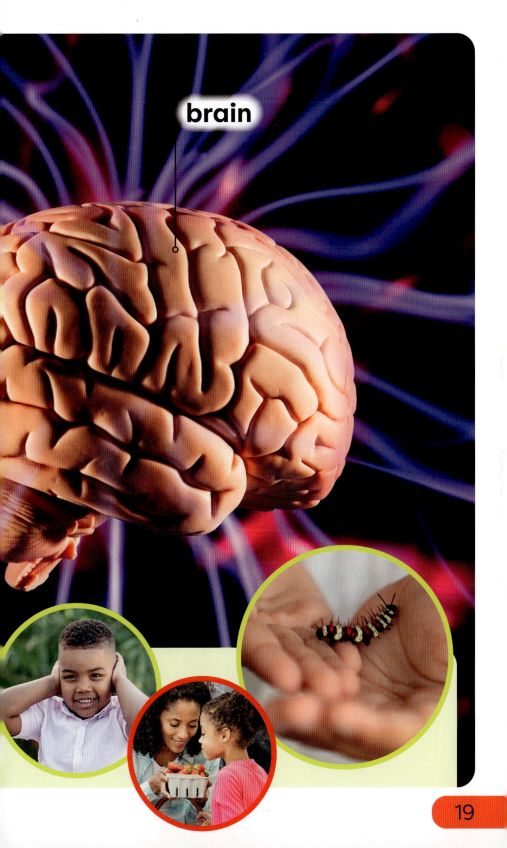

Senses are a team.
They work together.
They help us explore.

explore

Follow your senses! Discover the world around you.

Glossary

hear
to listen with your ears

see
to look at something with your eyes

smell
to sense odors with your nose

taste
to explore flavors with your mouth

touch
to feel something with your skin

Quiz

Answer the questions to see what you have learned. Check your answers with an adult.

1. What can eyes do?
2. What sense can fingers help with?
3. Which body part helps people hear?
4. Which body part do you use to smell?
5. What do you like to taste? What does it taste like?

1. See 2. Touch 3. Your ears 4. Your nose
5. Answers will vary